DAWN & DUSK WITH MY DOG

BOOK OF INSPIRING PHOTOS & QUOTES

Linda Shiffman

Alberta, Canada

Dedicated with love to my children:
Nathan, Aviva and Samara

In memory of Sasha
11/2016 - 04/2017

Her life was like her tail, much too short and sweet

Every new day presents new possibilities

INTRODUCTION

Sasha, a standard schnauzer puppy, came into our lives in early 2017 but after only a few short months of love and joy, she became ill. Sasha died of leukemia and her sudden death devastated our family. Cancer is insidious and it seems there are few who are not affected by its crippling claw. After a year of grieving for Sasha, we were fortunate to be gifted another schnauzer puppy, Nori, who is Sasha's half-sister and carries Sasha's spirit in her today.

Sadness touches all of our lives at one time or another. Having to take our puppy Nori for early morning walks allowed me time to reflect and quickly become inspired. While grieving for Sasha, I realized that I took for granted the simplest things. With Nori, I learned to be grateful for what I had instead of what I had lost. I began to look UP on my walks with Nori and I was rewarded every day with a different beautiful canvas of sky and clouds painted by the rays of the sun. I am not a professional photographer, just an incredibly fortunate person who happens to have a camera at the right place and time.

This book is a collection of my favorite photos taken from my walks with my dog along with some inspiring quotes. Photography can be different things to different people. For me, photos allow me to capture beautiful objects without stealing them, to freeze a fleeting moment that would otherwise be lost and to share them with everyone. I am grateful for the opportunity to see and capture so many beautiful things and I hope they make you smile.

A sunrise is like a warm kiss from the sun to the earth

We can be different and still be friends

It gets harder but you get better

Trust yourself

Turn your face to the sun and
the shadows fall behind you

Anonymous

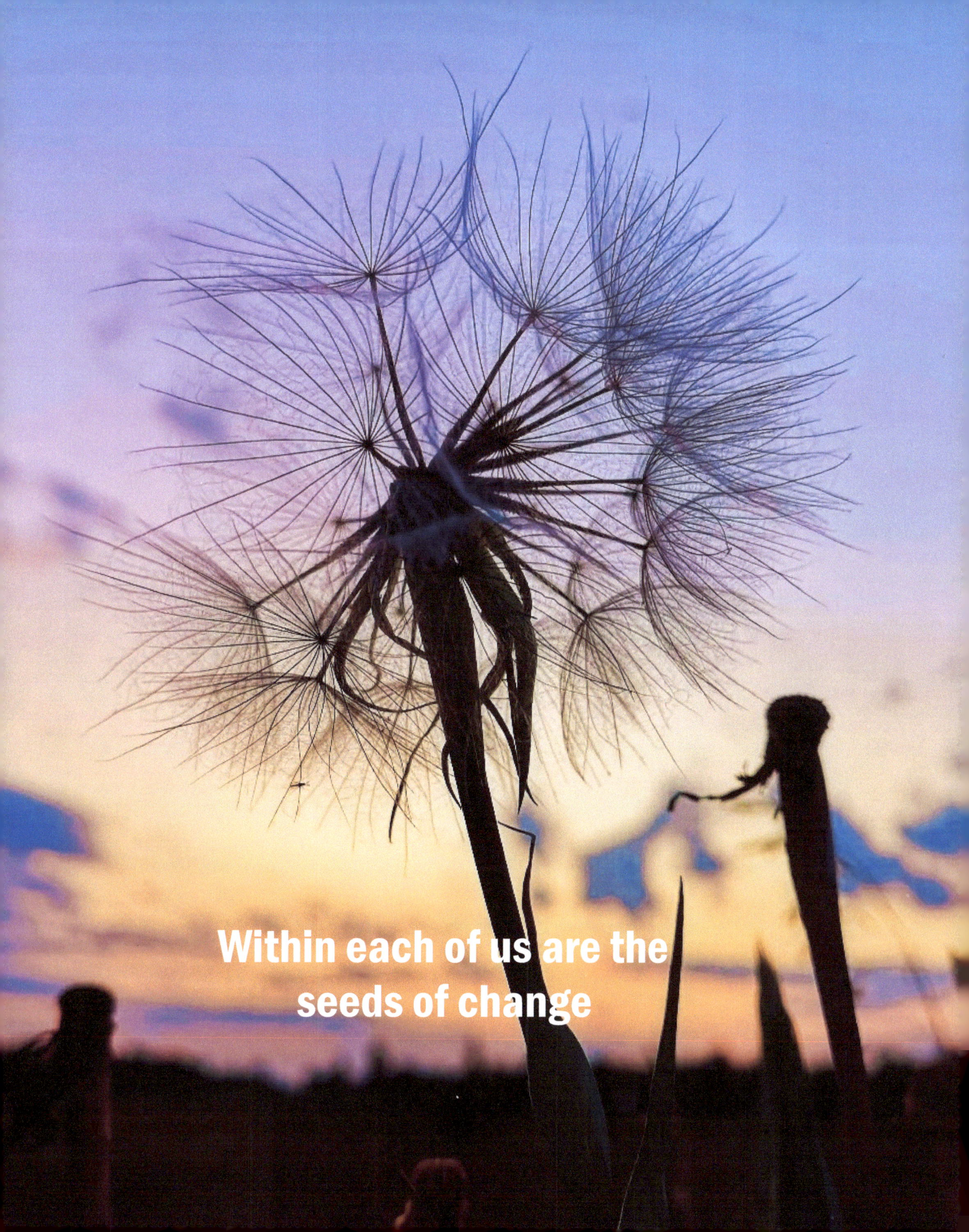
Within each of us are the
seeds of change

Three Sisters Mountain Range, Canmore, Alberta

We may not have it all together, but together we have it all

Anonymous

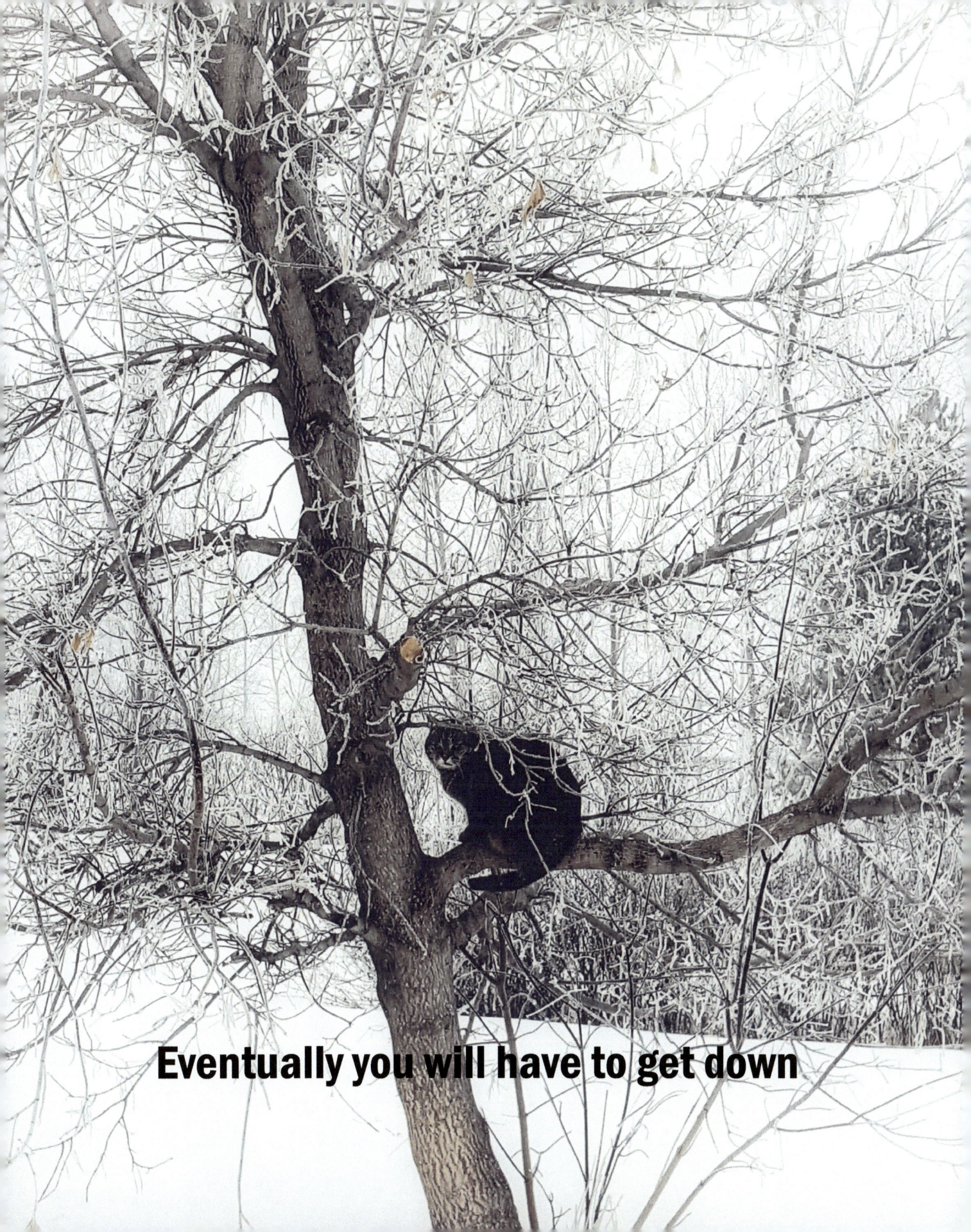

Eventually you will have to get down

Things look different in the light of day

Sun lifts fog off the river valley below, South Calgary

Keep flapping your wings &
you will get there

Without fire the Lodgepole pine cone
will not release its seeds

Give yourself a break

Stretch your limits

Sundog in the Alberta sky

A change in perspective can reveal a rare sight

Do your best today for a better tomorrow

Be grateful & have more than enough

Stalk of wheat, Southern Alberta

Inner beauty radiates long after physical beauty fades

No matter where you go

Mule deer rest at the foot of Three Sisters mountain range, Canmore

It is who you are with that matters

Deer along a country fence, South Calgary

Bee gathering nectar from wild sunflower

Dreams work when we work

Single ray of light can brighten all the darkness in the world

Anonymous

You are beautiful

Echinacea at sunset, South Calgary

There is nothing worth believing in more than YOU

Great things are on the horizon

Prairie hawk watches over Calgary

Your uniqueness is your strength

Bee Balm at sunset, South Calgary

The more you give, the more you get

To have something different,
do something different

Maple leaf, Ontario

Ripe Saskatoon berries, Southern Alberta

Change yourself for the better
Change the world for the better

Sun behind cloud creates a rainbow, Calgary

Without clouds there would be no rainbows

Perfection comes from persistence

Learn to dance in the rain instead of waiting for the storm to pass

Anonymous

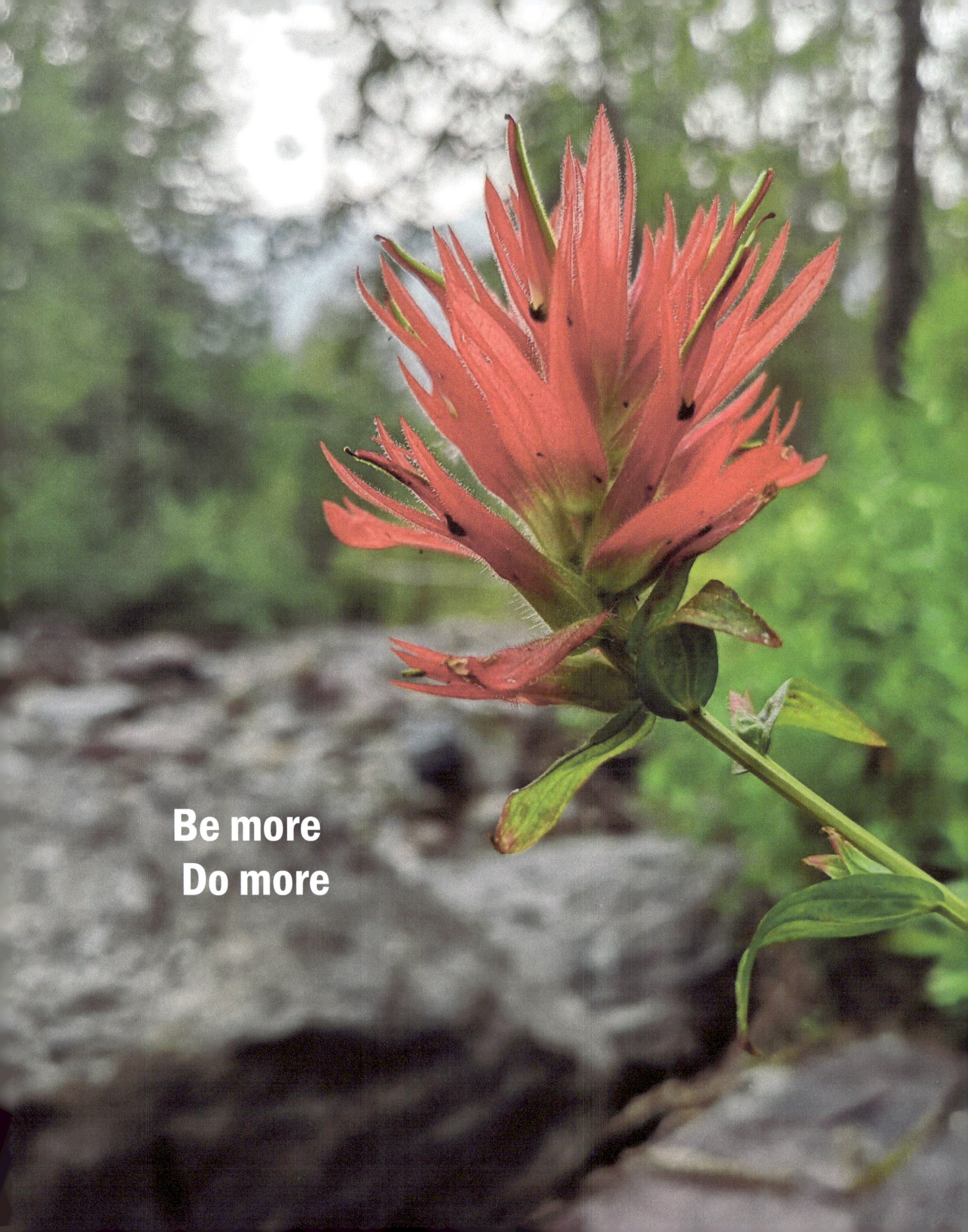

Be more
Do more

What looks like disappointment
may be opportunity

The question mark butterfly, polygonia interrogationis, looks like a dead leaf when its wings are closed

Waking up early to live a little more

The sunset is short

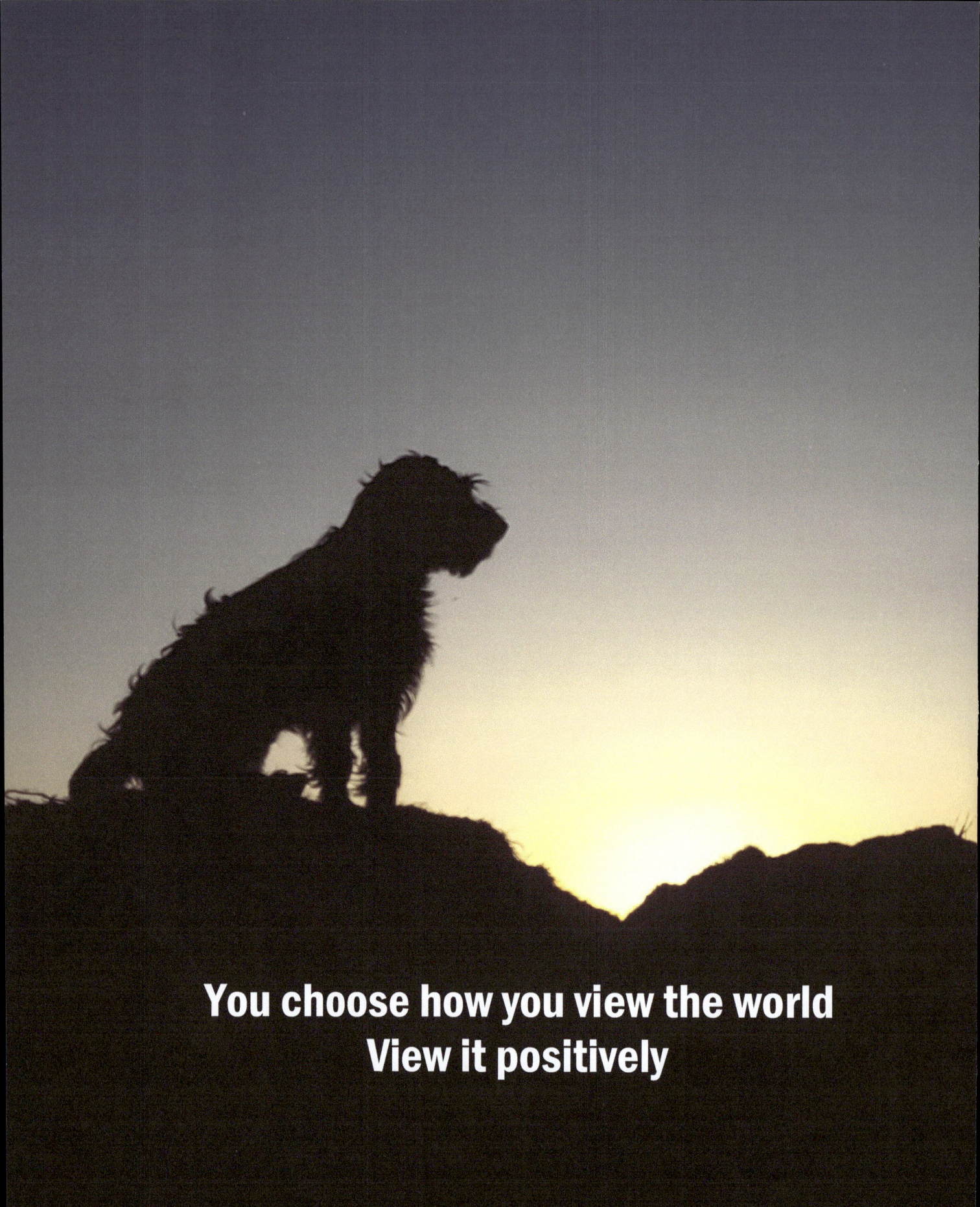

You choose how you view the world
View it positively

What you find is what you seek

You are stronger than you think

Anonymous

Drought tolerant lilac blooms fragrantly every spring, South Calgary

Tomorrow is a new day

However dark the night, dawn will break

-African Proverb

www.ingramcontent.com/pod-product-compliance
Lightning Source LLC
Chambersburg PA
CBHW041534090426
42744CB00022BA/21